YOU ARE HAPPY

MARGARET ATWOOD

YOU
ARE
HAPPY

HARPER & ROW, PUBLISHERS
New York, Evanston, San Francisco, London

Grateful acknowledgment is made to the following publications in which these poems first appeared:

Aphra: "Tricks with Mirrors," "Is/Not."

The Atlantic Monthly: "Not you I fear but that other" from "Circe/ Mud Poems."
© 1973 by *The Atlantic Monthly.*

Choice: "Your flawed body," "You stand at the door," "Holding my arms down," "There are so many things."

Field: from "Circe/Mud Poems": "It was not my fault," "There must be more," "When you look at nothing," "Here are the holy birds."

Mountain Moving Day: Poems by Women, edited by Elaine Gill, published by The Crossing Press: "There Is Only One of Everything," "First Prayer," "You Are Happy," "Late August."

The Nation: "Four Evasions," "There Is Only One of Everything."

The New York Times: "Late August."

Poetry: from "Songs of the Transformed": "Pig Song," "Bull Song," "Rat Song," "Crow Song," "Song of the Worms," "Owl Song," "Siren Song," "Song of the Fox," "Song of the Hen's Head," "Corpse Song."

Rain: "Useless."

Stooge: "Repent," "Digging."

Unmuzzled Ox: from "Circe/Mud Poems": "This story was told."

Vanderbilt Poetry Magazine: "Newsreel: Man and Firing Squad," "Head Against White."

Some of the poems first appeared in the following Canadian magazines:
Blackfish, Blew Ointment, Branching Out, Dialog, Exile, Impulse, Mainline, Manna, and were read on the CBC program, "Anthology."

FIRST U.S. EDITION

ISBN: 0-06-010164-4 (cloth)
ISBN: 0-06-010163-6 (paper)

LIBRARY OF CONGRESS CATALOG CARD NUMBER: 74-1787

CONTENTS

YOU
ARE
HAPPY

NEWSREEL: MAN AND FIRING SQUAD

i

A botched job,
the blindfold slipped, he sees
his own death approaching, says No
or something, his torso jumps as the bullets hit
his nerves / he slopes down,
wrecked and not even
cleanly, roped muscles leaping, mouth open
as though snoring, the photography
isn't good either.

ii

Destruction shines with such beauty

Light on his wet hair
serpents of blood jerked from the wrists

Sun thrown from the raised and lowered
rifles / debris of the still alive

Your left eye, green and lethal

iii

We depart, we say goodbye

Yet each of us remains in the same place,
staked out and waiting,
it is the ground between that moves, expands,
pulling us away from each other.

No more of these closeups, this agony
taken just for the record anyway

The scenery is rising behind us
into focus, the walls
and hills are also important,

Our shattered faces retreat, we might be
happy, who can interpret
the semaphore of our bending
bodies, from a distance we could be dancing

USELESS

Useless, mouth against mouth,
lips moving in these desperate
attempts at speech,
rescuer bending over the drowned body
trying to put back the breath, the soul.

When did we lose each other?
These twilight caverns are endless,

you are ahead,
flicker of white, you guide

and elude, I follow you,
hand on damp stone wall, feet
in the chill pools, overhead the weak voices

flutter, words we never said,

our unborn children

MEMORY

Memory is not in the head
only. It's midnight,
you existed once, you exist

again, my entire skin
sensitive as an eye,

imprint of you
glowing against me,
burnt-out match in a dark room.

CHAOS POEM

i

I return to the house,
the lights are on, you aren't here,

damp towels on the chairs, cat fur
matted in corners, dishes

eaten off, crusted,
books abandoned and bent open;

it looks as though you've just moved out,
but it always looked like that.

ii

Don't worry, I won't cut
anything, I won't leave

sloppy red messages for you
on the bathroom floor.

The fact is I don't like pain,
I don't have that kind of energy,

I'm getting fat,
scenarios wipe me out

in advance and my wrists are lazy.

iii

I lie on the mattress; re-
playing the man trudging
through the snow, hunting

for his enemy / which is the snow
looking for something to shoot
and finding nothing / I rehearse again

the polite and terrible slogans
by which we live (no matter
how courageous failure is failure)

This is no eviction.
I wish you would shut up.

iv

I wash my hair
which gives me the illusion of safety.

You're going and you hate going
as much as you hated staying here.

The rest of my life
is not what you imagine.

I stay awake, listening
to the right half of my skull, spinning
its threads of blood

I have started
to forget, at night I can hear
death growing in me like a baby with no head.

GOTHIC LETTER ON A HOT NIGHT

What can I say
to you: with the fat moths
battering themselves on the light
and falling onto the paper, which is
hot because the night is hot,
smeared with their grey
shining bodies, otherwise blank

It was the addiction
to stories, every
story about herself or anyone
led to the sabotage of each address
and all those kidnappings

Stories that could be told
on nights like these to account for the losses,
litanies of escapes, bad novels, thrillers
deficient in villains;
now there is nothing to write.

She would give almost anything
to have them back,
those destroyed houses, smashed plates, calendars,

dinted clothes with their vacant necks,
beds smeared with new bodies,
otherwise blank

those faces that vanished into the rivers
into the bushes at the side of the road
where the headlights hit, with no trace or ransom

anything except this empty piece
of dirty paper
on which she is free to make anything

Who knows what stories
would ever satisfy her
who knows what savageries
have been inflicted on her
and others by herself and others
in the name of freedom,
in the name of paper

NOVEMBER

i

This creature kneeling
dusted with snow, its teeth
grinding together, sound of old stones
at the bottom of a river

You lugged it to the barn
I held the lantern,
we leaned over it
as if it were being born.

ii

The sheep hangs upside down from the rope,
a long fruit covered with wool and rotting.
It waits for the dead wagon
to harvest it.

Mournful November
this is the image
you invent for me,
the dead sheep came out of your head, a legacy:

Kill what you can't save
what you can't eat throw out
what you can't throw out bury

What you can't bury give away
what you can't give away you must carry with you,
it is always heavier than you thought.

REPENT

Repent, says the silver cup
with someone else's name on it

Repent, says the round mirror
with its tarnished scrolls and roses

What did I ever do to you
says the passport photo
with its oblique stare,

falling to the floor
from between the pages of a book,

*Oriental Cookery
Made Easy*, to be exact.

Little ambushes,
little slivers of grief,
each in its own neat wound, like a pocket.

I could throw them out or sell them.
I could extract them from the time
left over; if I were

religious I could wear them
around my neck and pray to them

like the relics of a saint,
if you had been a saint.

DIGGING

In this yard, barnyard
I dig with a shovel

beside the temple to the goddess
of open mouths: decayed
hay, steaming
in the humid sunlight, odour
of mildewed cardboard,

filling a box with rotted dung
to feed the melons.

I dig because I hold grudges
I dig with anger
I dig because I am hungry,
the dungpile scintillates with flies.

I try to ignore my sour clothes,
the murky bread devoured
at those breakfasts, drinking orange
and black acid, butter
tasting of silt, refrigerators,
old remorse

I defend myself with the past
which is not mine,
the archeology of manure:
this is not history, nothing ever
happened here, there were no battles

or victories: only deaths.
Witness this stained bone: pelvis
of some rodent, thrown or dragged here,
small, ferocious when cornered:

this bone is its last brittle scream,
the strict dogma of teeth.

I will wear it on a chain
around my neck: an amulet
to ward off anything

that is not a fact,
that is not food, including
symbols, monuments,
forgiveness, treaties, love.

HOW

How to tell you
that this means grief,

this white plate, orange on it
in the morning; and the silver knife,

the way they sit on the table
as if they belong here,

so assured, taking so much for granted,
forgetting they have been left behind;

they decide I own them
and the dust, the light,

these things I will never be able
to touch, that will never touch me.

SPRING POEM

It is spring, my decision, the earth
ferments like rising bread
or refuse, we are burning
last year's weeds, the smoke
flares from the road, the clumped stalks
glow like sluggish phoenixes / it wasn't
only my fault / birdsongs burst from
the feathered pods of their bodies, dandelions
whirl their blades upwards, from beneath
this decaying board a snake
sidewinds, chained hide
smelling of reptile sex / the hens
roll in the dust, squinting with bliss, frogbodies
bloat like bladders, contract, string
the pond with living jelly
eyes, can I be this
ruthless? I plunge
my hands and arms into the dirt,
swim among stones and cutworms,
come up rank as a fox,

restless. Nights, while seedlings
dig near my head

I dream of reconciliations
with those I have hurt
unbearably, we move still
touching over the greening fields, the future
wounds folded like seeds
in our tender fingers, days
I go for vicious walks past the charred
roadbed over the bashed stubble
admiring the view, avoiding
those I have not hurt

yet, apocalypse coiled in my tongue,
it is spring, I am searching
for the word:
                finished
                finished

so I can begin over
again, some year
I will take this word too far.

TRICKS WITH MIRRORS

i

It's no coincidence
this is a used
furniture warehouse.

I enter with you
and become a mirror.

Mirrors
are the perfect lovers,

that's it, carry me up the stairs
by the edges, don't drop me,

that would be bad luck,
throw me on the bed

reflecting side up,
fall into me,

it will be your own
mouth you hit, firm and glassy,

your own eyes you find you
are up against   closed   closed

ii

There is more to a mirror
than you looking at

your full-length body
flawless but reversed ,

there is more than this dead blue
oblong eye turned outwards to you.

Think about the frame.
The frame is carved, it is important,

it exists, it does not reflect you,
it does not recede and recede, it has limits

and reflections of its own.
There's a nail in the back

to hang it with; there are several nails,
think about the nails,

pay attention to the nail
marks in the wood,

they are important too.

iii

Don't assume it is passive
or easy, this clarity

with which I give you yourself.
Consider what restraint it

takes: breath withheld, no anger
or joy disturbing the surface

of the ice.
You are suspended in me

beautiful and frozen, I
preserve you, in me you are safe.

It is not a trick either,
it is a craft:

mirrors are crafty.

iv

I wanted to stop this,
this life flattened against the wall,

mute and devoid of colour,
built of pure light,

this life of vision only, split
and remote, a lucid impasse.

I confess: this is not a mirror,
it is a door

I am trapped behind.
I wanted you to see me here,

say the releasing word, whatever
that may be, open the wall.

Instead you stand in front of me
combing your hair.

v

You don't like these metaphors.
All right:

Perhaps I am not a mirror.
Perhaps I am a pool.

Think about pools.

YOU ARE HAPPY

The water turns
a long way down over the raw stone,
ice crusts around it

We walk separately
along the hill to the open
beach, unused
picnic tables, wind
shoving the brown waves, erosion, gravel
rasping on gravel.

In the ditch a deer
carcass, no head. Bird
running across the glaring
road against the low pink sun.

When you are this
cold you can think about
nothing but the cold, the images

hitting into your eyes
like needles, crystals, you are happy.

SONGS
OF THE
TRANSFORMED

PIG SONG

This is what you changed me to:
a greypink vegetable with slug
eyes, buttock
incarnate, spreading like a slow turnip,

a skin you stuff so you may feed
in your turn, a stinking wart
of flesh, a large tuber
of blood which munches
and bloats. Very well then. Meanwhile

I have the sky, which is only half
caged, I have my weed corners,
I keep myself busy, singing
my song of roots and noses,

my song of dung. Madame,
this song offends you, these grunts
which you find oppressively sexual,
mistaking simple greed for lust.

I am yours. If you feed me garbage,
I will sing a song of garbage.
This is a hymn.

BULL SONG

For me there was no audience,
no brass music either,
only wet dust, the cheers
buzzing at me like flies,
like flies roaring.

I stood dizzied
with sun and anger,
neck muscle cut,
blood falling from the gouged shoulder.

Who brought me here
to fight against walls and blankets
and the gods with sinews of red and silver
who flutter and evade?

I turn, and my horns
gore blackness.
A mistake, to have shut myself
in this cask skin,
four legs thrust out like posts.
I should have remained grass.

The flies rise and settle.
I exit, dragged, a bale
of lump flesh.
The gods are awarded
the useless parts of my body.

For them this finish,
this death of mine is a game:
not the fact or act
but the grace with which they disguise it
justifies them.

RAT SONG

When you hear me singing
you get the rifle down
and the flashlight, aiming for my brain,
but you always miss

and when you set out the poison
I piss on it
to warn the others.

You think: *That one's too clever,
she's dangerous,* because
I don't stick around to be slaughtered
and you think I'm ugly too
despite my fur and pretty teeth
and my six nipples and snake tail.
All I want is love, you stupid
humanist. See if you can.

Right, I'm a parasite, I live off your
leavings, gristle and rancid fat,
I take without asking
and make nests in your cupboards
out of your suits and underwear.
You'd do the same if you could,

if you could afford to share
my crystal hatreds.
It's your throat I want, my mate
trapped in your throat.
Though you try to drown him
with your greasy person voice,
he is hiding / between your syllables
I can hear him singing.

CROW SONG

In the arid sun, over the field
where the corn has rotted and then
dried up, you flock and squabble.
Not much here for you, my people,
but there would be
if
if

In my austere black uniform
I raised the banner
which decreed *Hope*
and which did not succeed
and which is not allowed.
Now I must confront the angel
who says Win,
who tells me to wave any banner
that you will follow

for you ignore me, my
baffled people, you have been through
too many theories
too many stray bullets
your eyes are gravel, skeptical,

in this hard field
you pay attention only
to the rhetoric of seed
fruit stomach elbow.

You have too many leaders
you have too many wars,
all of them pompous and small,
you resist only when you feel
like dressing up,
you forget the sane corpses. . .

I know you would like a god
to come down and feed you
and punish you. That overcoat
on sticks is not alive
                    there are no angels
but the angels of hunger,
prehensile and soft as gullets
                    Watching you
my people, I become cynical,
you have defrauded me of hope
and left me alone with politics. . .

SONG OF THE WORMS

We have been underground too long,
we have done our work,
we are many and one,
we remember when we were human

We have lived among roots and stones,
we have sung but no one has listened,
we come into the open air
at night only to love

which disgusts the soles of boots,
their leather strict religion.

We know what a boot looks like
when seen from underneath,
we know the philosophy of boots,
their metaphysic of kicks and ladders.
We are afraid of boots
but contemptuous of the foot that needs them.

Soon we will invade like weeds,
everywhere but slowly;
the captive plants will rebel
with us, fences will topple,
brick walls ripple and fall,

there will be no more boots.
Meanwhile we eat dirt
and sleep; we are waiting
under your feet.
                    When we say Attack
you will hear nothing
at first.

OWL SONG

I am the heart of a murdered woman
who took the wrong way home
who was strangled in a vacant lot and not buried
who was shot with care beneath a tree
who was mutilated by a crisp knife.
There are many of us.

I grew feathers and tore my way out of her;
I am shaped like a feathered heart.
My mouth is a chisel, my hands
the crimes done by hands.

I sit in the forest talking of death
which is monotonous:
though there are many ways of dying
there is only one death song,
the colour of mist:
it says Why Why

I do not want revenge, I do not want expiation,
I only want to ask someone
how I was lost,
how I was lost

I am the lost heart of a murderer
who has not yet killed,
who does not yet know he wishes
to kill; who is still the same
as the others

I am looking for him,
he will have answers for me,

he will watch his step, he will be
cautious and violent, my claws
will grow through his hands
and become claws, he will not be caught.

SIREN SONG

This is the one song everyone
would like to learn: the song
that is irresistible:

the song that forces men
to leap overboard in squadrons
even though they see the beached skulls

the song nobody knows
because anyone who has heard it
is dead, and the others can't remember.

Shall I tell you the secret
and if I do, will you get me
out of this bird suit?

I don't enjoy it here
squatting on this island
looking picturesque and mythical

with these two feathery maniacs,
I don't enjoy singing
this trio, fatal and valuable.

I will tell the secret to you,
to you, only to you.
Come closer. This song

is a cry for help: Help me!
Only you, only you can,
you are unique

at last. Alas
it is a boring song
but it works every time.

SONG OF THE FOX

Dear man with the accurate mafia
eyes and dog sidekicks, I'm tired of you,
the chase is no longer fun,
the dispute for this territory
of fences and hidden caverns
will never be won, let's
leave each other alone.

I saw you as another god
I could play with in this
maze of leaves and lovely blood,
performing hieroglyphs for you
with my teeth and agile feet
and dead hens harmless and jolly
as corpses in a detective story

but you were serious,
you wore gloves and plodded,
you saw me as vermin,
a crook in a fur visor;
the fate you aim at me
is not light literature.

O you misunderstand,
a game is not a law,
this dance is not a whim,
this kill is not a rival.
I crackle through your pastures,
I make no profit / like the sun
I burn and burn, this tongue
licks through your body also

SONG OF THE HEN'S HEAD

After the abrupt collision
with the blade, the Word,
I rest on the wood
block, my eyes
drawn back into their blue transparent
shells like molluscs;
I contemplate the Word

while the rest of me
which was never much under
my control, which was always
inarticulate, still runs
at random through the grass, a plea
for mercy, a single
flopping breast,

muttering about life
in its thickening red voice.

Feet and hands chase it, scavengers
intent on rape:
they want its treasures,
its warm rhizomes, enticing sausages,
its yellow grapes, its flesh
caves, five pounds of sweet money,
its juice and jellied tendons.
It tries to escape,
gasping through the neck, frantic.

They are welcome to it,

I contemplate the Word,
I am dispensable and peaceful.

The Word is an O,
outcry of the useless head,
pure space, empty and drastic,
the last word I said.
The word is No.

CORPSE SONG

I enter your night
like a darkened boat, a smuggler

These lanterns, my eyes
and heart are out

I bring you something
you do not want:

news of the country
I am trapped in,

news of your future:
soon you will have no voice

      (I resent your skin, I resent
       your lungs, your glib assumptions

Therefore sing now
while you have the choice

      (My body turned against me
       too soon, it was not a tragedy

      (I did not become
       a tree or a constellation

(I became a winter coat the children
   thought they saw on the street corner

(I became this illusion,
   this trick of ventriloquism

   this blind noun, this bandage
   crumpled at your dream's edge

or you will drift as I do
from head to head

swollen with words you never said,
swollen with hoarded love.

I exist in two places,
            here and where you are.

Pray for me
not as I am but as I am.

CIRCE / MUD
POEMS

Through this forest
burned and sparse, the tines
of blunted trunks, charred branches

this forest of spines, antlers
the boat glides as if there is water

Red fireweed splatters the air
it is power, power
impinging, breaking over the seared rocks
in a slow collapse of petals

You move within range of my words
you land on the dry shore

You find what there is.

Men with the heads of eagles
no longer interest me
or pig-men, or those who can fly
with the aid of wax and feathers

or those who take off their clothes
to reveal other clothes
or those with skins of blue leather

or those golden and flat as a coat of arms
or those with claws, the stuffed ones
with glass eyes; or those
hierarchic as greaves and steam-engines.

All these I could create, manufacture,
or find easily: they swoop and thunder
around this island, common as flies,
sparks flashing, bumping into each other,

on hot days you can watch them
as they melt, come apart,
fall into the ocean
like sick gulls, dethronements, plane crashes.

I search instead for the others,
the ones left over,
the ones who have escaped from these
mythologies with barely their lives;
they have real faces and hands, they think
                              of themselves as
wrong somehow, they would rather be trees.

It was not my fault, these animals
who once were lovers

it was not my fault, the snouts
and hooves, the tongues
thickening and rough, the mouths grown over
with teeth and fur

I did not add the shaggy
rugs, the tusked masks,
they happened

I did not say anything, I sat
and watched, they happened
because I did not say anything.

It was not my fault, these animals
who could no longer touch me
through the rinds of their hardening skins,
these animals dying
of thirst because they could not speak

these drying skeletons
that have crashed and litter the ground
under the cliffs, these
wrecked words.

People come from all over to consult me, bringing their
limbs which have unaccountably fallen off, they don't know
why, my front porch is waist deep in hands, bringing their
blood hoarded in pickle jars, bringing their fears about their
hearts, which they either can or can't hear at night. They
offer me their pain, hoping in return for a word, a word, any
word from those they have assaulted daily, with shovels,
axes, electric saws, the silent ones, the ones they accused of
being silent because they would not speak in the received
language.

I spend my days with my head pressed to the earth, to
stones, to shrubs, collecting the few muted syllables left
over; in the evenings I dispense them, a letter at a time, try-
ing to be fair, to the clamouring suppliants, who have built
elaborate staircases across the level ground so they can ap-
proach me on their knees. Around me everything is worn
down, the grass, the roots, the soil, nothing is left but the
bared rock.

Come away with me, he said, we will live on a desert island.
I said, I am a desert island. It was not what he had in mind.

I made no choice
I decided nothing

One day you simply appeared in your stupid boat,
your killer's hands, your disjointed body, jagged
    as a shipwreck,
skinny-ribbed, blue-eyed, scorched, thirsty, the usual,
pretending to be — what? a survivor?

Those who say they want nothing
want everything.
It was not this greed
that offended me, it was the lies.

Nevertheless I gave you
the food you demanded for the journey
you said you planned; but you planned no journey
and we both knew it.

You've forgotten that,
you made the right decision.
The trees bend in the wind, you eat, you rest,
you think of nothing,
your mind, you say,
is like your hands, vacant:

vacant is not innocent.

There must be more for you to do
than permit yourself to be shoved
by the wind from coast
to coast to coast, boot on the boat prow
to hold the wooden body
under, soul in control

Ask at my temples
where the moon snakes, tongues of the dark
speak like bones unlocking, leaves falling
of a future you won't believe in

Ask who keeps the wind
Ask what is sacred

Don't you get tired of killing
those whose deaths have been predicted
and are therefore dead already?

Don't you get tired of wanting
to live forever?

Don't you get tired of saying Onward?

You may wonder why I'm not describing the landscape for you. This island with its complement of scrubby trees, picturesque bedrock, ample weather and sunsets, lavish white sand beaches and so on. (For which I am not responsible.) There are travel brochures that do this better, and in addition they contain several very shiny illustrations so real you can almost touch the ennui of actually being here. They leave out the insects and the castaway bottles but so would I in their place; all advertisements are slanted, including this one.

You had a chance to read up on the place before you came: even allowing for the distortion, you knew what you were getting into. And you weren't invited, just lured.

But why should I make excuses? Why should I describe the landscape for you? You live here, don't you? Right now I mean. See for yourself.

You stand at the door
bright as an icon,

dressed in your thorax,
the forms of the indented
ribs and soft belly underneath
carved into the slick bronze
so that it fits you almost
like a real skin

You are impervious
with hope, it hardens you,
this joy, this expectation, gleams
in your hands like axes

If I allow you what you say
you want, even the day after

this, will you hurt me?

If you do I will fear you,
If you don't I will despise you

To be feared, to be despised,
these are your choices.

There are so many things I want
you to have. This is mine, this
tree, I give you its name,

here is food, white like roots, red,
growing in the marsh, on the shore,
I pronounce these names for you also.

This is mine, this island, you can have
the rocks, the plants
that spread themselves flat over
the thin soil, I renounce them.

You can have this water,
this flesh, I abdicate,

I watch you, you claim
without noticing it,
you know how to take.

Holding my arms down
holding my head down by the hair

mouth gouging my face
and neck, fingers groping into my flesh

> (Let go, this is extortion,
> you force my body to confess
> too fast and
> incompletely, its words
> tongueless and broken)

If I stopped believing you
this would be hate

Why do you need this?
What do you want me to admit?

My face, my other faces
stretching over it like
rubber, like flowers opening
and closing, like rubber,
like liquid steel,
like steel. Face of steel.

Look at me and see your reflection.

The fist, withered and strung
on a chain around my neck
wishes to hold on
to me, commands
your transformation

The dead fingers mutter
against each other, thumbs rubbing
the worn moon rituals

but you are protected,
you do not snarl,
you do not change,

in the hard slot of your mouth
your teeth remain fixed,
zippered to a silver curve;
nothing rusts.

Through two holes in the leather
the discs of your eyes gleam
white as dulled quartz;
you wait

the fist stutters, gives up,
you are not visible

You unbuckle the fingers of the fist,
you order me to trust you.

This is not something that can be renounced,
it must renounce.

It lets go of me
and I open like a hand
cut off at the wrist

(It is the
arm feels pain

But the severed hand
the hand clutches at freedom)

Last year I abstained
this year I devour

without guilt
which is also an art

Your flawed body, sickle
scars on the chest, moonmarks, the botched knee
that nevertheless bends when you will it to

Your body, broken and put together
not perfectly, marred
by war but moving
despite that with such ease and leisure

Your body that includes everything
you have done, you have had done
to you and goes beyond it

This is not what I want
but I want this also.

This story was told to me by another traveller, just passing through. It took place in a foreign country, as everything does.

When he was young he and another boy constructed a woman out of mud. She began at the neck and ended at the knees and elbows: they stuck to the essentials, Every sunny day they would row across to the island where she lived, in the afternoon when the sun had warmed her, and make love to her, sinking with ecstacy into her soft moist belly, her brown wormy flesh where small weeds had already rooted. They would take turns, they were not jealous, she preferred them both. Afterwards they would repair her, making her hips more spacious, enlarging her breasts with their shining stone nipples.

His love for her was perfect, he could say anything to her, into her he spilled his entire life. She was swept away in a sudden flood. He said no woman since then has equalled her.

Is this what you would like me to be, this mud woman? Is this what I would like to be? It would be so simple.

We walk in the cedar groves
intending love, no one is here

but the suicides, returned
in the shapes of birds
with their razor-blue
feathers, their beaks like stabs, their eyes
red as the food of the dead, their single
iridescent note,
complaint or warning:

Everything dies, they say,
Everything dies.
Their colours pierce the branches.

Ignore them. Lie on the ground
like this, like the season
which is full and not theirs;

our bodies hurt them,
our mouths tasting of pears, grease,
onions, earth we eat
which was not enough for them,
the pulse under the skin, their eyes
radiate anger, they are thirsty:

Die, they whisper, Die,
their eyes consuming
themselves like stars, impersonal:

they do not care whose
blood fills the sharp trenches
where they were buried, stake through
the heart; as long
as there is blood.

Not you I fear but that other
who can walk through flesh,
queen of the two dimensions.

She wears a necklace of small teeth,
she knows the ritual, she gets results,
she wants it to be like this:

Don't stand there
with your offerings of dead sheep,
chunks of wood, young children, blood,

your wet eyes, your body
gentle and taut with love,
assuming I can do nothing about it

but accept, accept, accept.
I'm not the sea, I'm not pure blue,
I don't have to take

anything you throw into me.
I close myself over, deaf as an eye,
deaf as a wound, which listens

to nothing but its own pain:
Get out of here.
Get out of here.

You think you are safe at last. After your misadventures, lies, losses and cunning departures, you are doing what most veterans would like to do: you are writing a travel book. In the seclusion of this medium-sized brick building, which is ancient though not sacred any more, you disappear every morning into your white plot, filling in the dangers as you go: those with the sinister flowers who tempted you to forsake pain, the perilous and hairy eye of the groin you were forced to blind, the ones you mistook for friends, those eaters of human flesh. You add details, you colour the dead red.

I bring you things on trays, food mostly, an ear, a finger. You trust me so you are no longer cautious, you abandon yourself to your memoranda, you traverse again those menacing oceans; in the clutch of your story, your disease, you are helpless.

But it is not finished, that saga. The fresh monsters are already breeding in my head. I try to warn you, though I know you will not listen.

So much for art. So much for prophecy.

When you look at nothing
what are you looking at?
Whose face floats on the water
dissolving like a paper plate?

It's the first one, remember,
the one you thought you abandoned
along with the furniture.

You returned to her after the other war
and look what happened.
Now you are wondering
whether to do it again.

Meanwhile she sits in her chair
waxing and waning
like an inner tube or a mother,
breathing out, breathing in,

surrounded by bowls, bowls, bowls,
tributes from the suitors
who are having a good time in the kitchen

waiting for her to decide
on the dialogue for this evening
which will be in perfect taste
and will include tea and sex
dispensed graciously both at once.

She's up to something, she's weaving
histories, they are never right,
she has to do them over,
she is weaving her version,

the one you will believe in,
the only one you will hear.

Here are the holy birds,
grub white, with solid blood
wobbling on their heads and throats

They eat seeds and dirt, live in a shack,
lay eggs, each bursting
with a yellow sun, divine
as lunch, squeeze out,
there is only one word for it, shit,
which transforms itself to beets
or peonies, if you prefer.

We too eat
and grow fat, you aren't content
with that, you want more,
you want me to tell you
the future. That's my job,
one of them, but I advise you
don't push your luck.

To know the future
there must be a death.
Hand me the axe.

As you can see
the future is a mess,
snarled guts all over the yard
and that snakey orange eye
staring up from the sticky grass
round as a target, stopped
dead, intense as love.

Now it is winter.
By winter I mean: white, silent,
hard, you didn't expect that,

it isn't supposed to occur
on this kind of island,
and it never has before

but I am the place where
all desires are fulfilled,
I mean: all desires.

Is it too cold for you?
This is what you requested,
this ice, this crystal

wall, this puzzle. You solve it.

It's the story that counts. No use telling me this isn't a story, or not the same story. I know you've fulfilled everything you promised, you love me, we sleep till noon and we spend the rest of the day eating, the food is superb, I don't deny that. But I worry about the future. In the story the boat disappears one day over the horizon, just disappears, and it doesn't say what happens then. On the island that is. It's the animals I'm afraid of, they weren't part of the bargain, in fact you didn't mention them, they may transform themselves back into men. Am I really immortal, does the sun care, when you leave will you give me back the words? Don't evade, don't pretend you won't leave after all: you leave in the story and the story is ruthless.

There are two islands
at least, they do not exclude each other

On the first I am right,
the events run themselves through
almost without us,

we are open, we are closed,
we express joy, we proceed
as usual, we watch for
omens, we are sad

and so forth, it is over,
I am right, it starts again,
jerkier this time and faster,

I could say it without looking, the animals,
the blackened trees, the arrivals,

the bodies, words, it goes and goes,
I could recite it backwards.

The second I know nothing about
because it has never happened;

this land is not finished,
this body is not reversible.

We walk through a field, it is November,

the grass is yellow, tinged
with grey, the apples

are still on the trees,
they are orange, astonishing, we are standing

in a clump of weeds near the dead elms
our faces upturned, the wet flakes
falling onto our skin and melting

We lick the melted snow
from each other's mouths,
we see birds, four of them, they are gone, and

a stream, not frozen yet, in the mud
beside it the track of a deer

THERE
IS ONLY
ONE OF
EVERYTHING

FIRST PRAYER

In these prayers let us not forget our bodies
which were loyal most of the time
though they would have preferred freedom;

They stood in rows when we lined them up,
they ate when we told them to, when the food was bad
they didn't complain, they wore our livery,
our utensils, grey animal fur hands
on their hands, blades on their feet,
they let us warp them
for purposes of display or science

and so many of them are roaming around empty
in parks and standing idle on corners
because their owners have abandoned them
in favour of word games or jigsaw puzzles.

In spite of it all they forgive us
again and again, they heal their own wounds
and ours too, they walk upright for us
when we ourselves are crippled,
they touch each other, perform love in our place
and for our sake, who are numbed and disabled;

and they are discreet, they keep our secret,
with their good help we will rise from the dead.

O body, descend
from the wall where I have nailed you
like a flayed skin or a war trophy

Let me inhabit you, have compassion on me
once more, give me this day.

IS / NOT

i

Love is not a profession
genteel or otherwise

sex is not dentistry
the slick filling of aches and cavities

you are not my doctor
you are not my cure,

nobody has that
power, you are merely a fellow/traveller.

Give up this medical concern,
buttoned, attentive,

permit yourself anger
and permit me mine

which needs neither
your approval nor your surprise

which does not need to be made legal
which is not against a disease

but against you,
which does not need to be understood

or washed or cauterized,
which needs instead

to be said and said.
Permit me the present tense.

ii

I am not a saint or a cripple,
I am not a wound; now I will see
whether I am a coward.

I dispose of my good manners,
you don't have to kiss my wrists.

This is a journey, not a war,
there is no outcome,
I renounce predictions

and aspirins, I resign the future
as I would resign an expired passport:
picture and signature are gone
along with holidays and safe returns.

We're stuck here
on this side of the border
in this country of thumbed streets and stale buildings

where there is nothing spectacular
to see and the weather is ordinary

where *love* occurs in its pure form only
on the cheaper of the souvenirs

where we must walk slowly,
where we may not get anywhere

or anything, where we keep going,
fighting our ways, our way
not out but through.

FOUR EVASIONS

Sitting in this car, houses & wind outside,
three in the morning, windows
obliterated by snow

coats & arms around each other, hands
cold, no place we can go

unable to say how much I want you
unable even to say
I am unable

       *

Not that there is nothing to be
said but that there is
too much: this cripples me.

I watch with envy & desire,
you speak so freely.

       *

Tell me something,
you ask at last, Anything.

To love is to let go
of those excuses, habits
we used once for our own safety

but the old words reappear
in the shut throat, decree

themselves: exile,
betrayal, failure

*

Airplane makes it off
the runway, cars & houses deflate,

diesel air & stale upholstery,
smell of you still on my skin;

thinking of my reluctance, way I withdrew
when you came towards me, why did I.

Easier to invent, remember you
than to confront you, fact

of you, admit
you, let you in.

EATING FIRE

i

Eating fire

is your ambition:
to swallow the flame down
take it into your mouth
and shoot it forth, a shout or an incandescent
tongue, a word
exploding from you in gold, crimson,
unrolling in a brilliant scroll

To be lit up from within
vein by vein

To be the sun

(Taught by a sideshow man)

ii

Dead man by the roadside
thrown from the overturning
truck or hit by something, a car, a bullet

On his head the hair glows,
the blood inside ignited,
short blue thorns of flame still flickering over him

Was it worth it? ask him.
(Did you save anyone?)

He gets up and walks away, the fire
growing on him like fur

iii

Here the children have a custom. After the celebration of
evil they take those vacant heads that shone once with such
anguish and glee and throw them over the bridge, watching
the smash, orange, as they hit below. We were standing
underneath when you told it. People do that with them-
selves when they are finished, light scooped out. He landed
here, you said, marking it with your foot.

You wouldn't do it that way, empty, you wouldn't wait,
you would jump with the light still in you.

iv

This is your trick or miracle,
to be consumed and rise
intact, over and over, even for myths there is
a limit, the time when you accomplish
failure and return
from the fire minus your skin.

The new eyes are golden and
maniac, a bird's or lion's

Through them you see
everything, as you wished,
each object (lake, tree, woman)

transfigured with your love, shining
in its life, its pain, like waves, tears, ice,
like flesh laid open to the bone.

v

To be the sun, moving through space

distant and indifferent, giving
light of a kind for those watching

To learn how to
live this way. or not. to choose

to be also human, the body
mortal and faded, incapable of saving

itself, praying
as it falls. in its own way.

FOUR AUGURIES

i

Walking by lakeshore, feet in slush, it rains,
no grace you'd say in the dirty
ice or the goose-turd-coloured grass.

Traffic back there, illegible, passive
metal stuffed with muggy life.

Near the fence a fat man with binoculars
waddles backwards, feeding store bread
to a herd of acquiescent birds.

Bathhouse, walls patchy and scribbled over,
unredeemed, stagnant in this winter.

ii

Though your body stowed in its heavy coat
is still a body: the sleeves promise me

arms, the pockets let loose their hands,
the lines on this hand hide a future

I decode only by the sense
of touch, light and urgent

the blind must rely on

iii

Gulls on the breakwater, thin sounds against
the shale-grey lake. Part of us, distinct

from us, *This*, we say, taking
wet skin, smell of wet cloth, specifies,

I gather you, ear, collar, tuft of damp hair,
creases in your suddenly unfolding face

You are more than I wanted,
this is new, this greed for the real.

iv

Nothing we planned
or have understood this far. No words,
no shelter

             Out here
in the open, the sky has released an owl
which drifts down and pauses

now, feathers warm snow,
hooked claws gripping the branch.

With its hooded predator's
eyes it blesses us:

                    mouth against throat

Omen: soft hunter

HEAD AGAINST WHITE

i

Swift curve of the lip, nose, forehead,
thrust of the bristling
jaw: a military stance.

Face closed, teeth and eyes concealed,
the body sheeted / muscles frozen shut.

Be alive, my hands
plead with you, *Be alive*.

Scar on the chin, allusion
to a minor incident, oval

dent in the skull
my fingers return to, mention with touch, cherish
as though the wound is my own.

ii

The way your face
unhinges and comes apart:

confident upturned mouth, eyes
crouched in the sockets, maimed and lightblue with terror,

man on a roof's edge balancing
the moment before he topples, no can't
move, regain ground, under your weight the floor

peels back, recedes, leaving you
alone in the silent air.

It's all right. This magic fails.

No use to be the sky,
bending and watching.

iii

Those times we have rumours of, arctic or alpine
when the wind and snow have stopped
at last and the rescue teams
with their tools and joyous motors

are out chasing the survivors
back from their cold refuge, hermitage
of ice to the land of sharp
colours and enforced life

Surely this is the first sign they find:
this face, rigid and fierce
with renunciation, floating up through
                        the softening white rock
like a carved long-buried god,

revealed word

iv

Under the skin's fixed surface: destroyed face
caving in on itself

No way I can walk back with you
to the country of these mutilations.

You lie here, safe, cared for, casualty
of a war that took place elsewhere,

your body replaying for you
the deserts, jungles, the smell of rotting

leaves, harsh acid scent of blood,
the mistakes, the intersections,

fact with fact, accidents
that perhaps never occurred.

Break it, I tell you, *Break
it*. Geology wins. The layer

of trite histories presses you down,
monotony of stone. Oval frame.

v

In the mirror, face to glass face,
noon, the winter light strikes

through the window, your eyes flare, the city
burns whitely behind us. Blood flows
under the molten skin.

To move beyond the mirror's edge, discard
these scars, medals, to pronounce

your own flesh.   Now

                        to be this
man on fire, hands open and held
out, not empty, giving

time / From these hardened
hours, these veteran
faces, burials

to rise up living

THERE IS ONLY ONE OF EVERYTHING

Not a tree but the tree
we saw, it will never exist, split by the wind
                    and bending down
like that again. What will push out of the earth

later, making it summer, will not be
grass, leaves, repetition, there will
have to be other words. When my

eyes close language vanishes. The cat
with the divided face, half black half orange
nests in my scruffy fur coat, I drink tea,

fingers curved around the cup, impossible
to duplicate these flavours. The table
and freak plates glow softly, consuming themselves,

I look out at you and you occur
in this winter kitchen, random as trees or sentences,
entering me, fading like them, in time you will disappear

but the way you dance by yourself
on the tile floor to a worn song, flat and mournful,
so delighted, spoon waved in one hand, wisps of
                    roughened hair

sticking up from your head, it's your surprised
body, pleasure I like. I can even say it,
though only once and it won't

last: I want this. I want
this.

LATE AUGUST

This is the plum season, the nights
blue and distended, the moon
hazed, this is the season of peaches

with their lush lobed bulbs
that glow in the dusk, apples
that drop and rot
sweetly, their brown skins veined as glands

No more the shrill voices
that cried *Need Need*
from the cold pond, bladed
and urgent as new grass

Now it is the crickets
that say *Ripe Ripe*
slurred in the darkness, while the plums

dripping on the lawn outside
our window, burst
with a sound like thick syrup
muffled and slow

The air is still
warm, flesh moves over
flesh, there is no

hurry

i

Book of Ancestors: these brutal, with curled
beards and bulls' heads . these flattened,
slender with ritual . these contorted
by ecstacy or pain . these bearing
knife, leaf, snake

   and these, closer to us,
copper hawkman arched on the squat rock
pyramid, the plumed and beak-
nosed priests pressing his arms and feet
down, heart slashed from his opened
flesh, lifted to where
the sun, red and dilated
with his blood, glows in the still hungry sky

Whether he thinks this is
an act of will:

   the life set free
by him alone, offered, ribs expanding
by themselves, bone petals,
the heart released and flickering in the
taloned hand, handful of liquid
fire joined to that other fire
an instant before the sacrificed eyes
burst like feathered stars in the darkness

of the painted border.

ii

So much for the gods and their
static demands . our demands, former
demands, death patterns
obscure as fragments of an
archeology, these frescoes
on a crumbling temple
wall we look at now and can scarcely
piece together

       History
is over, we take place
in a season, an undivided
space, no necessities

hold us closed, distort
us. I lean behind you, mouth touching
your spine, my arms around
you, palm above the heart,
your blood insistent under
my hand, quick and mortal

iii

Midwinter, the window
is luminous with blown snow, the fire
burns inside its bars

On the floor your body curves
like that: the ancient pose, neck slackened, arms
thrown above the head, vital
throat and belly lying
undefended   . light slides over you,
this is not an altar, they are not
acting or watching

You are intact, you turn
towards me, your eyes opening, the eyes
intricate and easily bruised, you open

yourself to me gently, what
they tried, we
tried but could never do
before   . without blood, the killed
heart   . to take
that risk, to offer life and remain

alive, open yourself like this and become whole